Cooking With Kids

Recipes for Year-Round Fun

by Tania Kourempis-Cowling

illustrated by Corbin Hillam

Fearon Teacher Aids
A Division of Frank Schaffer Publications, Inc.

Dedication

A special thank you to my children Michael, Tina, and Christopher whose love, help, and taste-testing made this book possible.

Editors: Cindy Barden and Janet Barker
Cover and Interior Design: Good Neighbor Press, Inc.
Illustrator: Corbin Hillam

Fearon Teacher Aids products were formerly manufactured and distributed by American Teaching Aids, Inc., a subsidiary of Silver Burdett Ginn, and are now manufactured and distributed by Frank Schaffer Publications, Inc. FEARON, FEARON TEACHER AIDS, and the FEARON balloon logo are marks used under license from Simon & Schuster, Inc.

Fearon Teacher Aids
A Division of Frank Schaffer Publications, Inc.
23740 Hawthorne Boulevard
Torrance, CA 90505

Table of Contents

The Ultimate Learning Experience

What combines art, math, reading, creative thinking, science, sensory experiences, and social skills, and results in delightful treats for friends and family? Cooking!

Cooking is full of opportunities for learning. It is the type of activity that can be part of a child's education, both at home and in the classroom.

Cooking exposes children to a variety of sensory and cognitive experiences. Children can see how food changes before their eyes. An egg becomes hard and rubbery after it is boiled. They learn to read recipes and measure ingredients.

Children can smell the aroma of foods and have many opportunities to feel different textures from soft squishy pudding to hard, crunchy carrots. Call children's attention to hearing the different sounds of food, like the pop of popping corn and the crunch of fresh celery. Last but not least, children can taste different foods and enjoy the flavor.

Cooking also provides social opportunities and helps children develop social skills, like the importance of cooperation and sharing in a group. Selecting a recipe, gathering ingredients, taking turns stirring, pouring, chopping, and dicing can be a group effort. Cooking and serving meals and treats focuses around friends and family.

There is an art to cooking. Children use creativity as they find new ways to combine ingredients and make up new recipes. There are many opportunities to design, decorate, and display food in an appealing manner. Food presentation is so important—what looks good, tastes good!

Cooking With Kids is a creative design cookbook. Here you will find seasonal and holiday ideas to create fun and tasty sandwiches, salads, snacks, and desserts.

As teachers, include cooking as part of your curriculum. As parents, enjoy spending quality time with your children. You can enhance holidays and everyday meals by *Cooking With Kids.*

iv

Safety Precautions

Wash hands before handling food.

Do not allow anyone with open sores to handle food.

Find alternate activities for children with colds. They can read the recipe or be observers for the day.

Use low tables for work surfaces at a height children can reach. If your counters are too high, use a card table.

Never allow children to stand on chairs to reach cooking surfaces or to watch stove-top cooking.

Always turn handles toward the back of the stove when cooking on top of a stove.

Whenever possible, use microwave ovens, toaster ovens, or electric skillets on a table at the child's level. Remind children that these utensils are very hot.

Provide enough tools and utensils for all children to participate. Use unbreakable bowls and utensils whenever possible.

When using a vegetable peeler, teach children to scrape away from themselves.

Provide blunt knives or serrated plastic knives for children to use when cutting soft foods, like cooked eggs, bananas, and cooked potatoes.

Make sure an adult supervises at all times.

Identify children with food allergies. Give them a different project that will not involve foods they cannot eat or modify recipes so they can eat them.

In the event of a minor burn, run cold water over the area immediately.

In the event of a minor cut, wash the area thoroughly and apply a bandage immediately.

1

Football Salad

It's kick-off time. Watch your favorite team play and enjoy a football salad at half time.

What you need for each salad:

Leaf of lettuce, washed and dried
1 hard-boiled egg
3 carrot strips
Black olives cut into small strips

What you do:

1. Arrange three carrots strips on a lettuce leaf in the shape of a goal post.

2. Cut the hard-boiled egg in half lengthwise.

3. Place one egg half in the center of the goal post, round side up.

4. Decorate the egg half with strips of black olives to look like football lacing.

Popcorn Medley

Mix any or all of the following ingredients together. Fill snack bags and tie the ends closed with seasonal colored yarn, ribbon or raffia.

What you need:

Popped popcorn
Raisins
Sunflower nuts (seeds)
Dried fruit chunks

Nuts
Puffed cereal
Pumpkin seeds
Mini pretzel twists

Apple Peanut Butter Rounds

Many varieties of apples are available in the fall. Buy different types and let children try slices of several kinds to compare the colors, tastes, textures, and smells.

What you need:

An apple
Creamy or crunchy peanut butter
Spoon and knife
Wax paper

What you do:

1. Remove the core from an apple.

2. Fill the hollowed-out center core with peanut butter.

3. Wrap the apple in wax paper and refrigerate for about an hour.

Before serving, slice the apple into horizontal rounds. You will have apple slices with a filled peanut butter center.

Option: Use cheese spread instead of peanut butter to fill the center of the apple.

Sandwich Puzzles

Celebrate back to school with peanut butter and jelly sandwiches that are fun to make and eat. No more ho-hum when children eat these sandwiches.

What you need:

Bread
Peanut butter
Jelly
Other fillings. See ideas below.

What you do:

1. Make a peanut butter and jelly sandwich.

2. Cut the sandwich into zig-zag pieces to form a puzzle.

Serve the sandwich pieces on a plate and have children put the puzzle together before eating this snack or lunch.

Other great sandwich fillings:

Peanut butter and banana slices
Peanut butter and bacon
Peanut butter and raisins
Peanut butter and apple butter
Peanut butter and honey
Peanut butter and cheese
Jelly and raisins
Jelly and banana slices

Traffic Lights

As children make and eat these treats, talk about what the red, yellow, and green lights on a traffic light mean and why it is important to obey traffic light rules.

What you need:

Graham crackers
Vanilla frosting
M & M™ candies (red, yellow, and green)

What you do:

1. Separate the graham cracker into rectangular sections.

2. Frost the graham crackers.

3. Place candies on the frosted graham crackers in the order of a traffic light: red, yellow, and green.

Columbus Boat Sandwiches

Columbus sailed the ocean blue in 1492. Celebrate Columbus Day with Columbus Boat Sandwiches. The crew never had it so good!

What you need:

Oval dinner rolls
Tuna salad, egg salad, or other filling
American cheese slices
Toothpicks

What you do:

1. Slice the tops off the dinner rolls and hollow a pocket.

2. Fill the rolls with tuna salad, egg salad, or another filling of your choice.

3. Cut the sliced cheese diagonally to form two triangles.

4. Weave a toothpick through the cheese slice and poke it into the filling to make the boat's sail.

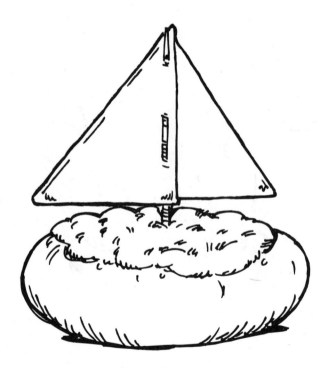

Apples and Honey

Rosh Hashana, the Jewish New Year, is celebrated during the month of September. Apples dipped in honey are one of the traditional foods eaten during this holiday to symbolize a sweet year.

What you need:

Apples wedges
Honey

What you do:

Let children dip apple wedges in a bowl of honey and enjoy this sweet snack.

Sand-Witches

These Halloween sandwiches are fun for children to make and cute to eat. Share cut-off crusts with the birds in your backyard or at the park.

What you need for each Sand-Witch:

    2 slices of bread
    Sandwich filling
    Small lettuce leaves
    Carrot
    Pickle spear
    Olives

What you do:

1. Spread children's favorite filling between two slices of bread.

2. Place the sandwich on the plate so that the most pointed side is toward the top. The top sides with the crust will be the hair line.

3. Cut the crusts from adjacent sides. This part will be the face.

4. Add small lettuce leaves on each side of the "face," tucked into the sandwich slightly for the hair.

5. Decorate the face with olive slice eyes, a pickle mouth, and a long carrot nose.

Jack-o-Lantern Rice Cakes

No messy pumpkins to clean and carve to create Jack-O-Lantern Rice Cakes. These Halloween treats are fun to make and great after-school snacks.

What you need:

Rice cakes
Whipped cream cheese
Red and yellow food coloring
Raisins
Mini-pretzels (optional)

What you do:

1. Place cream cheese in a bowl. Tint it orange using two drops of red and three drops of yellow food coloring. Mix thoroughly.

2. Spread orange cream cheese on a rice cake.

3. Have the children make jack-o-lantern faces using raisins.

4. Use mini-pretzels to outline the eyes. (optional)

9

Flaming Eyes Cake

Want to create a real sensation at a Halloween party? Watch the excitement on children's faces as you present them with this Flaming Eyes dessert.

What you need:

A frosted cake (previously baked or store-bought)
2 empty, thoroughly-cleaned eggshell halves
2 sugar cubes
Lemon extract
Matches
Decorative foods for facial features (optional)

What you do:

1. Place clean empty eggshell halves on top of the cake to represent eyes. The hollow part of the shell should be face-up.

2. Add other decorations for the nose, mouth, ears, or hair, like candied cherries, raisins, pretzels, or gum drops, if desired.

3. Soak two sugar cubes in lemon extract. Place one sugar cube in each egg shell.

When it's time to serve the cake, light the sugar cubes with a match. Wait for the flames to extinguish themselves before serving. Adult supervision is needed.

Vegetable Cornucopia

A cornucopia, also called a horn of plenty, is traditionally filled with vegetables from the harvest. In this case, however, children can eat the cornucopia as well as the veggies inside.

What you need for the cornucopia:

Ice cream cones (pointed sugar cones)
Cut vegetables: carrot sticks, broccoli, cauliflower, cherry tomatoes, etc.

What you need for the dip:

8 ounces sour cream
1 package dry onion soup or ranch-style mix

What you do:

1. Fill each ice cream cone with cut vegetables.
2. Combine sour cream and dry onion soup or ranch-style mix.

   Chill and serve. Children will enjoy dunking their veggies in the dip.

Apple Turkeys

Serve chilled Apple Turkeys for dessert, as an appetizer, or for a fun gobbley snack. You probably won't have many leftovers!

What you need:

Apples
Toothpicks (Use round, colored toothpicks, if possible)
Cheese chunks
Olives
Fruit chunks
Piece of posterboard (to draw a turkey head)

What you do:

1. Fill toothpicks with chunks of cheese, fruit, and olives. These will be the turkey's tail feathers.

2. Insert toothpick tail feathers into the back of the apple.

3. Draw and cut out a turkey head shape from posterboard. Make a slit in the front of the apple and insert the head.

12

Ice Cream Snowballs

Celebrate winter with Ice Cream Snowballs. Even if it never snows where you live, you can enjoy this kind of snowball. These treats are easy to make and fun to eat.

What you need:

Vanilla ice cream
Flaked coconut
Ice cream scoop
Cupcake liners

What you do:

1. Roll a round scoop of vanilla ice cream in a small bowl of flaked coconut.

2. After the snowball is coated, place it in a paper cupcake liner.

3. Store snowballs in the freezer until you are ready to serve.

Birdseed Biscuits

Let children pretend they are winter birds enjoying their seeds as they eat these delicious biscuits. Save the crumbs if there are any, and put them out for the real winter birds to enjoy.

What you need:

    Can of refrigerator biscuits
    Melted margarine or butter
    Sesame seeds and/or sunflower nuts

What you do:

1. Place the biscuits on a cookie sheet or pan as directed on the package label.

2. Brush the tops of the biscuits with melted butter or margarine. Press seeds on the top of each biscuit.

3. Bake as directed.

    Serve warm with jam or honey.

Holiday Pizza Faces

When your Holiday Pizza Face is ready, let everyone admire the details before slicing. You might even take a photo before your creation is nothing but a memory.

What you need:

Frozen pizza(s)
Decorative foods: salami strips, pepperoni slices, red and green pepper strips, onion slices, cherry tomatoes, green or black olives, etc.

Note: If you can find frozen, individual-size pizzas, let each child create his or own holiday pizza face.

What you do:

1. Use decorative foods creatively to make faces on the pizza(s) before baking. Try making a snowman, reindeer, Santa, or Elf face. You might even try making a picture of yourself!
2. Bake the pizza according to the package directions.

Christmas Candles

For a light holiday dessert, serve individual Christmas candles to friends and family.

What you need for each candle:

2 round pineapple slices
Banana
Red maraschino cherry

What you do:

For the candle holder:
Place a pineapple ring on a plate.

For the candle:
Cut the end tips from a banana. Stand the banana inside the pineapple ring.

For the handle:
Cut a small portion of a pineapple ring and lean it along the side of the banana.

For the flame:
Place a maraschino cherry
on top of the banana.

Menorah Sandwiches

Celebrate Hanukkah with Menorah Sandwiches for lunch or a snack.

What you need for each sandwich:

Slice of bread
10 pretzel sticks
Candy corn or small cinnamon candy
Creamy peanut butter

What you do:

1. Spread a slice of bread with creamy peanut butter.

2. Arrange nine pretzel sticks in a row on the peanut butter to look like candles. The pretzel in the center needs to be taller than the others. Add a half pretzel stick to it to represent the Shamash.

3. Top each "candle stick" with a candy corn or small cinnamon candy for the flame.

Delicious **Latkes** *Family Favourite*

Serve this special Hanukkah treat with applesauce or sour cream.

What you need:

1 grated onion
1 teaspoon salt
1 egg
6 medium potatoes (peeled and grated)
3 tablespoons flour, matzoh meal, or bread crumbs
½ teaspoon baking powder
Vegetable oil

What you do:

1. Combine onion, salt, egg, and potatoes. Beat well.

2. Mix the remaining ingredients and beat into the potato mixture.

3. Drop dough by spoonfuls in hot oil in a frying pan or electric skillet. Brown latkes on both sides. Adult supervision is necessary.

4. Drain and serve.

✳ Cook/fry like pancakes

Chocolate Confetti Candy

Celebrate New Year's with Chocolate Confetti Candy. Then make a resolution to serve these treats for birthday parties and other holidays all year long.

What you need:

Bag of chocolate chips (semisweet or milk chocolate)
Peanuts and/or raisins
Candy sprinkles/confetti
Wax paper

What you do:

1. Place the chocolate chips in a bowl and microwave for one to two minutes, until melted.

2. Stir in peanuts or raisins or both if desired.

3. Drop the mixture by spoonfuls onto a wax paper-lined cookie sheet.

4. Sprinkle with decorative candy confetti or sprinkles.

5. Refrigerate until firm.

6. Place candies in a bowl and serve at a cool room temperature.

19

Crispy Cheese Balls

Serve these cheese appetizers with the Lucky Party Punch at your New Year's party. You'll find the punch recipe on the next page.

What you need:

    1 cup grated cheddar cheese
    4 ounces margarine, softened
    1 cup flour
    1 cup Rice Krispies™ cereal

What you do:

1. Mix softened margarine and cheese together.

2. Mix in remaining ingredients.

3. Form the dough into marble-size balls.

4. Place dough balls on an ungreased cookie sheet.

5. Bake at 350° for 10 to 15 minutes until golden brown.

Lucky Party Punch

Red has traditionally been a lucky color to the people of China. They use many red items and decorations for their New Year's celebration.

What you need for each serving of punch:

1 cup strawberry soda
1 scoop strawberry ice cream
Maraschino cherries

What you do:

1. Combine soda and ice cream in a glass.
2. Garnish with cherries.

   Serve with a spoon and a straw.

CHERRIE

Easy Fried Rice

Celebrate Chinese New Year with this easy fried rice recipe.

What you need:

4 cups cooked rice
2 to 3 tablespoons soy sauce
½ cup cooked meat (beef, pork, or chicken)
2 chopped green onions or scallions
2 eggs
2 tablespoons vegetable or sesame oil

What you do:

1. Scramble the eggs. Set aside.

2. Stir-fry the meat and onions. Set aside.

3. Heat two tablespoons of oil in a large frying pan.

4. Add the cooked rice. Cook until it is heated throughout. Stir frequently.

If the rice is too dry, add a little water and cover the pan to steam the rice.

5. Add the other ingredients to the pan with the rice.

6. Stir in the soy sauce.

This recipe makes about 10 to 12 small servings.

Stuffed Bananas

Kwanzaa is an African-American holiday that begins on December 26 and ends on January 1. This holiday commemorates traditional African harvest festivals. One of the favorite African fruits is the banana. Let children make these stuffed bananas and enjoy this delicious warm desert.

What you need for each stuffed banana:

Banana
Chocolate chips
Mini-marshmallows

What you do:

1. Peel the banana and place it on a piece of wax paper.

2. With a spoon or table knife, carve an opening along the top side (like a pocket opening) of the banana.

3. Fill the pocket with chocolate chips and mini-marshmallows.

4. Wrap wax paper around the banana and microwave it for about 30 seconds: long enough to melt the chocolate and marshmallows.

If you use a conventional oven, wrap the bananas in aluminum foil.

*We would do these at our Girl Guide camps when I was a teenager in 1969 cooking them in coals from our campfire
♡ Babcia

Kwanzaa Flag Cookies

Help children make flag cookies that display the colors of Kwanzaa; red, black, and green.

What you need:

Graham crackers
Vanilla frosting
Food coloring

What you do:

1. Divide white frosting into three bowls. Add red food coloring to one and green to another. Combine a mixture of red, green, blue, and yellow food coloring to make black in the third bowl.

2. Spread a stripe of each color on the graham cracker to make a flag. (The red stripe goes on top, the black in the middle, and the green at the bottom.)

24

Pizza Hearts

What could be better than edible Valentines for your friends and family? Make plenty. Children love them! Make your Valentine's Day meal complete by serving Pink Milk Shakes.

What you need:

Slices of white or whole wheat bread
Pizza sauce
Shredded mozzarella cheese
Heart-shaped cookie cutter

What you do:

1. Cut heart shapes from slices of toasted bread using a cookie cutter.
2. Spread with pizza sauce and sprinkle with shredded mozzarella cheese.
3. Broil until cheese melts.

Pink Milk Shakes

What you need:

10 ounces frozen strawberries
4 cups cold milk

What you do:

1. Combine milk and strawberries in a blender.
2. Blend until smooth.
3. Serve with straws decorated with heart stickers.

Irish Spud Dessert

This desert resembles a baked potato with sour cream and chives, a staple in every Irish home. The twist is that this potato is deliciously sweet to eat!

What you need:

Chocolate ice cream
Whipped cream or whipped topping
Flaked coconut
Green food coloring
Ice cream scoop

What you do:

1. Press two round scoops of chocolate ice cream together to look like a baked potato.

2. Refreeze until firm.

3. Scoop out a pocket on top and fill with whipped cream or topping.

4. Tint coconut with a drop or two of green food coloring. Sprinkle green coconut on top of whipped cream.

5. Freeze until ready to serve.

Shamrock Shakes

Everyone is Irish on St. Patrick's Day. Celebrate with a Shamrock Shake.

What you need:

1 banana
2 cups lime sherbet
2 cups milk
Green paper cups (optional)
Straws
Shamrocks cut from green construction paper

What you do:

1. Blend ingredients together until smooth.

2. Cut shamrocks from green construction paper and attach them to straws with small pieces of tape. Serve Shamrock Shakes in green paper cups with a shamrock straw.

Mud Cake with Worms

It's spring! Celebrate with a mud cake full of worms. For a special treat, let children eat the mud cake with small, clean plastic sand shovels!

What you need:

Bag of unfrosted chocolate cookies
½ stick melted butter
1 pint vanilla ice cream
Fudge sauce
Gummy worms

What you do:

1. Place cookies in resealable plastic bags. Have children crush the cookies by rolling over the bags with a rolling pin.

2. Place cookie crumbs in a bowl and mix with melted butter.

3. Press the mixture into a glass 8" x 8" (20 cm x 20 cm) cake dish. (Double the recipe to make a larger cake).

4. Soften the ice cream. Layer it onto the crumb crust.

5. Spread ice cream with fudge topping.

6. Decorate the cake with gummy worms.

7. Put the cake in the freezer until firm. Keep frozen until ready to serve.

28

3-D Animals

Make a zoo of three-dimensional animals and parade them across the table. 3-D animals are a fun snack for children to make and eat.

What you need:

   Animal crackers
   Peanut butter
   Jam or jelly

What you do:

1. Give each child three crackers of the same animal.

2. Have them spread peanut butter and jam or jelly on the crackers to make three-layer animal sandwich cookies.

   Stand the cookies up and view the zoo before the children begin to chomp away. This is one time when children will be hungry enough to eat an elephant!

Fluffy Cloud Potatoes

April showers usually bring May flowers, but not in this case.
You won't get any showers from these Fluffy Cloud Potatoes.

What you need:

Instant mashed potatoes
Toppings: bacon bits, shredded cheese, chives, etc.

What you do:

1. Prepare instant potatoes according to package directions.
2. Let children take a few spoonfuls of potatoes and spread them on their plates to resemble fluffy clouds.
3. Sprinkle toppings on potatoes and enjoy potato clouds for a spring snack or lunch.

Hard-Boiled Bunnies

What will you serve for breakfast on Easter morning? How about making Hard-Boiled Bunnies? Not only will you have a breakfast fit for an Easter Bunny, you can also use up some of the eggs you colored!

What you need for each bunny:

1 hard-boiled egg
Lettuce leaf
Carrot
Red pepper
Black olives

What you do:

1. Carefully peel a hard-boiled egg. Slice the egg lengthwise.

2. Place one-half of the hard-boiled egg on a lettuce leaf with the yolk side down.

3. Slice the other half of the hard-boiled egg into halves to form bunny ears. Arrange them on the leaf above the first half.

4. Make bunny faces on the egg. Use olive slices for eyes, a piece of red pepper for the nose, and thin carrot strips for whiskers.

Serve plain or with dressing.

Breakfast Bunnies

Here's a treat to go with your Hard-Boiled Bunnies. Try this twist on plain old French toast for your Easter breakfast.

What you need:

6 to 8 slices of white or wheat bread
2 eggs
½ cup milk
1 tablespoon sugar
¼ teaspoon cinnamon
Dash of salt
Margarine or butter
Syrup
Bunny-shaped cookie cutter

What you do:

1. Use a cookie cutter to cut bunny shapes from bread.

2. Beat eggs. Add milk, sugar, cinnamon and salt. Mix well.

3. Heat a griddle or frying pan to medium-high heat. Grease the pan with margarine. Dip the bunny bread in the egg mixture coating both sides.

4. Place the egg-coated bunny bread on a griddle and brown on both sides. Adult supervision is necessary.

5. Serve warm with syrup.

Candy-Coated Matzoh

During this eight-day holiday (Passover) in the spring, Jewish families are restricted from certain foods and sweets. This is a fun way to decorate Matzoh (one of the main foods of this holiday) and create an artistic dessert.

What you need:

Matzoh crackers
Chocolate chips (kosher, optional) or colored chocolate meltable rounds
Clean cotton swabs or clean paintbrushes

What you do:

1. Melt the chocolate chips or candy pieces in a microwave oven or in a double boiler on top of the stove.

2. Use the paintbrushes or cotton swabs to "paint" melted chocolate pictures and designs on this popular cracker.

Admire the artwork and enjoy this sweet treat.

Cone Sandwiches

May Day is also known as a Basket Day. Traditionally, people delivered baskets of flowers and treats to friends and family to celebrate May Day.

What you need:

Flat-bottom ice cream cones (not sugar cones)
Sandwich filling: tuna, chicken or ham salad

What you do:

Fill the ice cream cone with children's favorite sandwich filling and serve for lunch or snack.

For a pretty topping, add an edible flower for color. Check with your local florist. There are some varieties of flowers used for cooking.

Flower Pot Dessert

Celebrate May Day by inserting a beautiful garden flower inside the straw when you serve this Flower Pot Dessert.

What you need:

Gelatin dessert
Plastic cups
Straws
Flowers (fresh or paper)

What you do:

1. Prepare gelatin dessert according to package directions. Fill individual small plastic cups about half full.

2. Refrigerate until gelatin is nearly set.

3. Cut a straw in half. Poke the straw in the gelatin and return to the refrigerator until gelatin is firm.

4. Insert a fresh flower in the straw before serving.

Pastel Thumbprint Cookies

Children can make these personalized cookies for mom on Mother's Day.

What you need for the cookies:

Refrigerator sugar cookie roll

What you need for the frosting:

3 to 4 tablespoons water
2 cups powdered sugar
½ teaspoon vanilla
Pinch of salt
Food coloring

What you do to make the cookies:

1. Cut the sugar cookie roll into ½ inch slices and place on a cookie sheet.
2. Have children make a thumbprint in the center of each cookie. *(Clean hands only!)*
3. Bake as directed.
4. Make the frosting while the cookies cool.

What you do to make the frosting:

1. Combine sugar, vanilla, and salt. Add water, one tablespoon at a time, until the mixture is smooth and creamy.
2. Divide the frosting into several small bowls. Tint each bowl a different pretty pastel color using food coloring.
3. Dab a little bit of frosting into each thumb indentation.

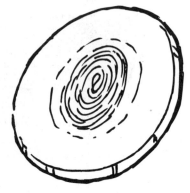

Lady's Parfait

Serve this delightful parfait to Mom for breakfast on Mother's Day.

What you need for each parfait:

Clear plastic glass
Cornflakes cereal
Sliced strawberries
Vanilla yogurt
1 whole strawberry

What you do:

1. Layer the cereal, yogurt, and strawberries in the clear glass. Repeat the layers until the glass is full.

2. Garnish with a whole strawberry on top.

Mexican Nachos

Celebrate Cinco de Maya (the fifth of May) with Mexican nachos.

What you need:

Tortilla chips
Can of refried beans
Grated cheese
Salsa

What you do:

1. Arrange a layer of tortilla chips on a plate.

2. Drop a rounded teaspoon of refried beans on each chip.

3. Cover the beans with grated cheese.

4. Microwave until cheese melts.

5. Serve with salsa.

Mexican Buffet

Set your table with small bowls of some or all of the fillings suggested. Give each child a round tortilla. Children can combine fillings to create their own super Mexican meals.

Suggestions for fillings:

Ground beef
Shredded chicken
Refried beans
Salsa
Picante sauce
Guacamole
Shredded cheeses
Chopped tomatoes
Sour cream
Diced red and green peppers
Minced jalapenos
Sliced black olives
Shredded lettuce
Diced red onions

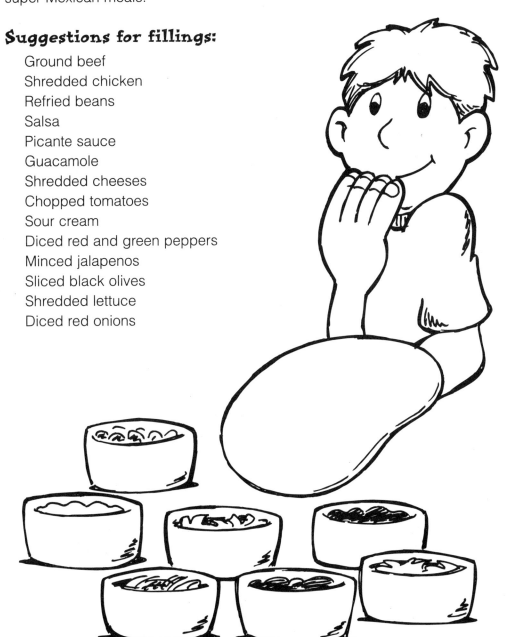

Clown Cake

Everybody loves a clown, so make everyone extra happy by making this Clown Cake. It's guaranteed to produce lots of giggles.

What you need:

One-layer round yellow cake
Vanilla frosting
Variety of candies to decorate the face
Cloth or paper bow tie for decoration
Flaked coconut
Food coloring

What you do:

1. Prepare a round, one-layer yellow cake or purchase one already baked, but not frosted.

2. Spread vanilla frosting on top of the cake.

3. Use different kinds of candy or candied fruit to create a clown's face.

4. Mix a few drops of food coloring with flaked coconut to give it a bright color. Sprinkle the coconut around the top of the face for hair.

5. Add a paper or cloth bow tie at the bottom of the plate to finish the clown look.

40

Butterfly Salad

Celebrate summer with a beautiful butterfly salad.

What you need for each salad:

Carrot stick
Olive
Lettuce leaf
Pear halves: canned or fresh
Raisins and or small cinnamon candies

What you do:

1. Place a carrot stick in the center of a lettuce leaf. This is the butterfly's body.

2. Add an olive to the top of the carrot stick for its head.

3. Arrange two pear halves along the sides of the carrot stick for the butterfly wings.

4. Decorate the wings with raisins or small cinnamon candies.

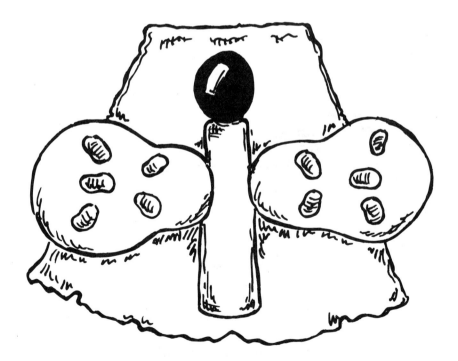

Hot Dog Racers

Make dad a special lunch for Father's Day. Treat him to a Hot Dog Racer.

What you need for each racer:

Hot dog
Bun
4 round carrot slices
Olive
Toothpicks
2 red pimentos

What you do:

1. Place a cooked hot dog in a bun.

2. Add four carrot slices to the outside of the bun for wheels.

3. Prick an olive with a toothpick. Stick it into the hot-dog at the far edge to represent the driver.

4. Add two red pimentos to the back of the bun for the tail lights.

The Candy Man

Make a Father's Day card and give dad this creative edible on his special day.

What you need:

1 small box of novelty candy or a small box of raisins
4 candy rolls, like Sweet Tarts™ or Tootsie Rolls™
1 lollipop
Tape

What you do:

1. Tape a lollipop to the back of a box of candy or raisins. The lollipop is the head and the box is the body.

2. Tape two rolls of candy to the box for the arms. Attach two rolls of candy for the legs.

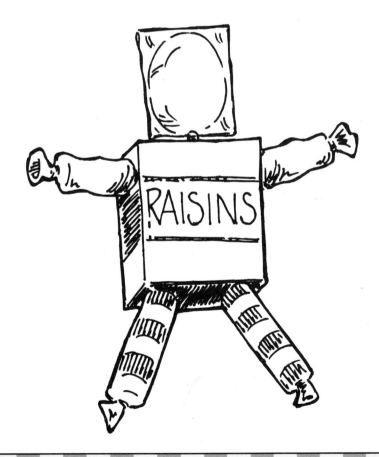

43

Patriotic Pinwheels

Celebrate the Fourth of July with Patriotic Pinwheels. Add flag toothpicks to show your patriotism. Serve with All-American Lemonade. Hurrah for the red, white and blue!!

What you need for each Pinwheel:

Slice of bread
Peanut butter
Red jam or jelly
Fancy toothpick or flag toothpick

What you do:

1. Cut the crusts off the bread.
2. Cut the bread into two strips. Spread one with peanut butter and the other with red jam or jelly.
3. Place one strip of bread on top of the other with the filling sides up.
4. Roll the strips into a pinwheel and secure it with a fancy toothpick.

All-American Lemonade

What you need:

1 can frozen lemonade
1 liter bottle of ginger ale
1 small bottle red maraschino cherries
Blueberries
Ice cube tray and water

What you do:

1. Make special ice cubes by placing a few blueberries into each section of an ice cube tray. Fill with water and freeze.
2. Prepare frozen lemonade according to directions.
3. Mix lemonade with ginger ale in a punch bowl.
4. Add cherries and frozen blueberry ice cubes.